Story of the Vikings Coloring Book

by A. G. Smith

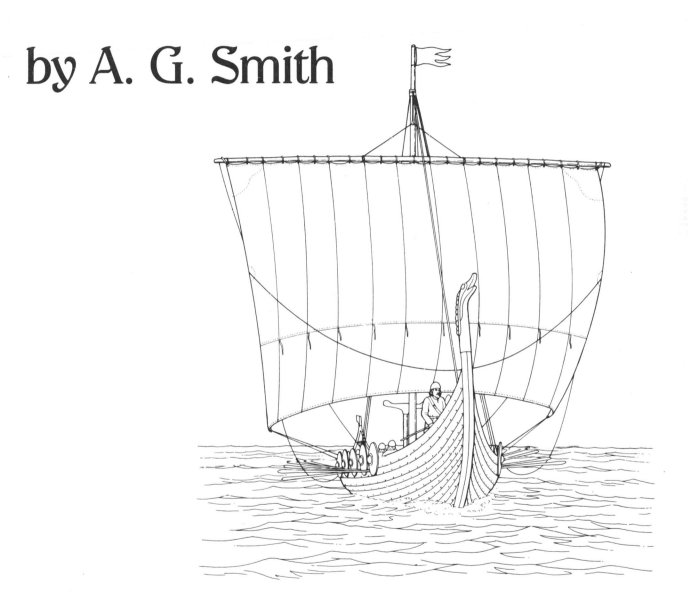

DOVER PUBLICATIONS, INC., New York

For Joan Magee

Published in Canada by General Publishing Company, Ltd.,
30 Lesmill Road, Don Mills, Toronto, Ontario.
Published in the United Kingdom by Constable and Company, Ltd.

Story of the Vikings Coloring Book is a new work, first published by
Dover Publications, Inc., in 1988.

DOVER *Pictorial Archive* SERIES

International Standard Book Number: 0-486-25653-7

Manufactured in the United States of America
Dover Publications, Inc., 31 East 2nd Street, Mineola, N.Y.
11501

Introduction

One of the most colorful periods in history was the Viking age (roughly 800–1100 A.D.), when the Scandinavian peoples entered the international scene in an unparalleled burst of activity—often violent. During this period, the nations of Denmark, Norway and Sweden were molded out of small chieftaincies and principalities, and became Christian realms. Iceland, Greenland and a section of North America were colonized by Norsemen, who also raided and settled in parts of the British Isles and northwestern mainland Europe. Viking traders and dynasts loomed large on Russian soil. Scandinavian mercenaries served the Byzantine emperors; Scandinavian merchants trafficked with the caliphs of Baghdad.

To the Christianized, sedentary Frankish, Anglo-Saxon and Irish chroniclers, the first Vikings seemed to be murderous demons who had appeared out of nowhere, and this is the romantic reputation that they have retained in the popular memory. Actually, the Scandinavians, northernmost and most remote of the Germanic peoples, were merely still in a phase of historical development that the other Germanic groups, and the continental Celts, had already passed through and largely forgotten: the Heroic Age. A multitude of mutually hostile local warlords—with retinues of fighting men personally loyal to them, and with court bards to praise their valor and curse their enemies—ruled over a much larger population of farmers and herdsmen (with some admixture of slaves, either purchased or captured in combat).

The Scandinavian region was already fairly prosperous in late Roman times, thanks to its iron ore and furs, and enjoyed far-flung trade relations, as archaeological excavations have shown. (For the whole history of Scandinavia through Viking times, archaeology has proved to be a more reliable source of knowledge than either the unsympathetic and incomplete reports made by the Vikings' victims and enemies, or even than the Old Norse sagas, which were written centuries after the events they chronicle and freely mix fantasy with fact.) The early "dark ages," characterized by wholesale migrations of populations, were disruptive in Scandinavia as elsewhere, but international trade continued and beautiful works of art were created (see the helmet on page 33). By about 800, various social and economic pressures at home combined with favorable outward circumstances to bring about the great Viking explosion whose political, technological and artistic results are recorded in the pictures and captions of the *Story of the Vikings Coloring Book.*

Although this book follows the common practice of using the term "Vikings" loosely as a synonym of the Scandinavians or Norsemen of the period, actually it should strictly be applied only to those individuals who set out on raiding expeditions in quest of plunder and adventure, temporarily leaving behind them their regular employment as farmers or the like. The etymology of "Viking" is disputed, like so much else pertaining to these people. The information in the present book makes use of the most recent generally shared opinions of recognized authorities in the field. After a view of the Norse homeland (page 5), the Vikings' ships—chief instruments of their success as raiders and traders—are pictured and described on pages 6 through 13. Pages 14 through 32 provide a survey of the military and political history of the age, including a number of famous voyages, battles and other events. The last part of the book, pages 33 through 48, is devoted to the everyday life and the arts and crafts of the Vikings: weaponry, metalwork, carving on wood and stone, religion, runes, literature and other aspects of this fascinating era.

The homelands of the Norsemen, or Vikings, were in Scandinavia (present-day Denmark, Norway and Sweden) and on the islands of the Baltic Sea. In many areas, the land available for cultivation was just a narrow strip on the shores of fjords, mountain-enclosed inlets of the sea—as in this Norwegian scene. Overpopulation, limited opportunities at home and a worsening of the climate have all been suggested as reasons for the overseas expansion that ushered in the Viking Age about 800 A.D.

It was the Vikings' ships that made their expansion possible. As shipbuilders they were unsurpassed at the time. Over centuries they developed ships with true keels and with hulls of lapstrake (or clinker) construction—overlapping planks riveted together—combining strength with flexibility. The shallow draft of these ships enabled them to land on almost any beach and to sail far up inlets and rivers, allowing startling surprise attacks.

The relative lightness of the Viking ships made it possible for them to be portaged (hauled overland) around rapids or between bodies of water, as in this scene of Viking activity in Russia in the ninth century.

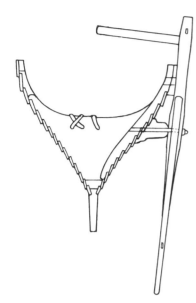

THE VIKING SHIP

Based on the 76-foot-long mid-ninth-century ship discovered in 1880 at Gokstad, Norway, and now in the Viking Ship Museum in Oslo

Steering Board

Viking ships were steered by a rudder located on the right side of the ship rather than at the stern. It was attached by a rope or thong. The term starboard ("steering side") for the right side of a ship is derived from this arrangement.

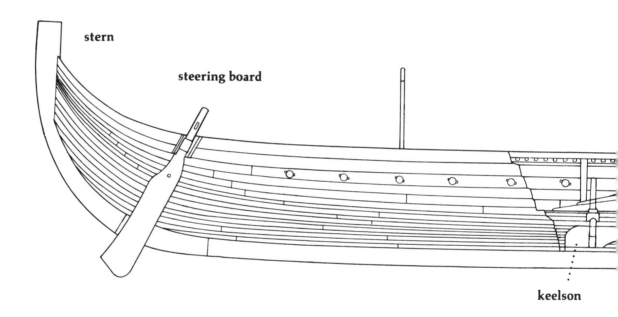

stern

steering board

keelson

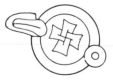

oar-hole cover

rigging block

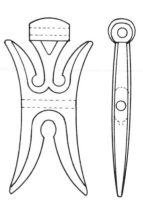

Lapstrake (or Clinker) Construction

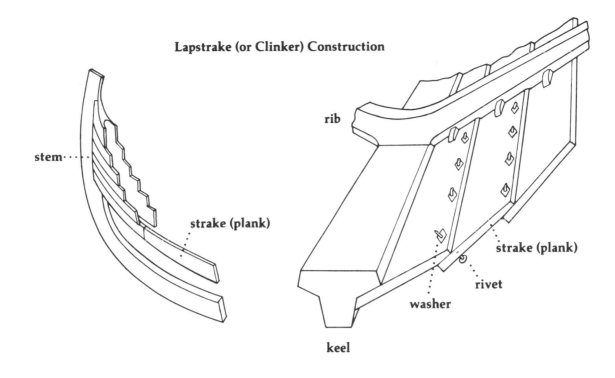

stem

strake (plank)

rib

strake (plank)

rivet

washer

keel

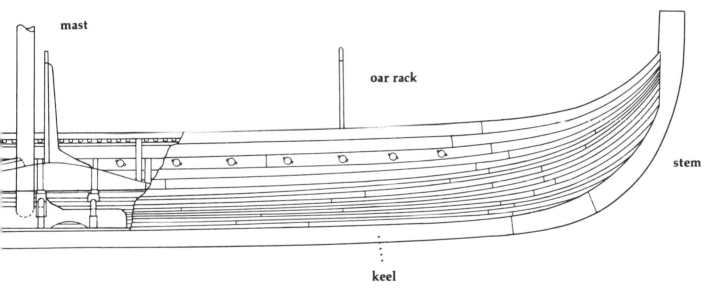

mast

oar rack

stem

keel

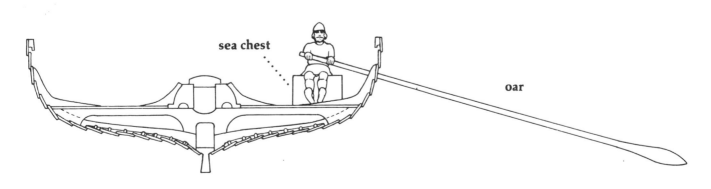

sea chest

oar

Frame System

The Vikings were fearless sailors, even braving the treacherous North Atlantic in open ships. It has been said that the Vikings' true home was the sea.

12

Viking navigators did not possess compasses, but calculated their position on the open sea by the sun or the stars. They were also aided by a bearing dial and a stick with the sun's position marked at significant latitudes. The Vikings also took soundings, measuring off the line by their arm span; the term "fathom" for this six-foot length is derived from the Norse word for it.

Though there had been Viking activity on English coasts somewhat earlier, their lightning raid for plunder on the monastery island of Lindisfarne (now called Holy Island) off the Northumbrian coast in 793 shocked the civilized world and awakened the European West to the significance of the Viking presence. Raids on northern England, Scotland and Ireland continued into the ninth century. These

early forays were pirate raids carried out by lesser chieftains. As consolidation of forces and the beginnings of national states progressed in Denmark, Norway and Sweden, regular armies left Scandinavia for the British Isles and raiding gave way to military occupation and civilian settlement.

By 851 the Vikings were already occupying parts of England, their success there being abetted by the division of the territory among the rival dynasties of Wessex, Mercia, East Anglia and Northumbria. After severe setbacks, Alfred the Great (reigned 871–899) of Wessex, the southernmost kingdom, defeated the Vikings at Edington in 878, thus saving the south for the Anglo-Saxons. By the ensuing treaty (shown above) the Viking army leader Guthrum withdrew to East Anglia, thus rounding out the already partially constituted Danelaw, as the Vikings' large portion of England came to be known.

16

The Vikings were colonists as well as warriors. As early as the end of the eighth century they were already setting in the Orkney, Shetland and Hebrides Islands off the coasts of Scotland. Livestock raising and fishing were the principal livelihoods. The illustration shows the stone and turf farm buildings of Jarlshof in the Shetlands. (The Norse-style name, meaning "nobleman's farm," was invented by Sir Walter Scott; actually the site had been in use since the Bronze Age, well before the time of Christ.)

By the end of the ninth century the Vikings had colonized the Faeroe Islands. They were settling in Iceland by about 860. That island, which had scarcely been populated earlier, was soon full of prosperous farms with sod-built houses. The illustration shows such a farmhouse at Stöng, where a modern reconstruction exists. During the same century the Vikings were also settling in Ireland (Dublin, Cork and elsewhere) and at York in northern England.

18

In 930 Iceland became a republic, of which the chief political institution was the annual Althing ("general assembly"), in which 36 of the leading islanders met to establish laws and settle disputes. They met in an encampment at Thingvellir ("assembly plain"), a rocky ridge at the edge of a grassy plain in southwestern Iceland. This drawing, which shows a "lawspeaker" holding forth at the foot of Law Rock, is based on an 1873 painting by the English artist W. G. Collingwood. Iceland lost its independence to Norway in 1262.

Viking raids on France, with deep penetration via major rivers, began in the 840s. Eventually Norse armies wintered in France, as they did in England. The most striking event in France was the unsuccessful Viking siege of Paris (then basically just the Île de la Cité and the Latin Quarter) in 885 (shown in the illustration). The greatest Norse success came in 911, when the Viking chieftain Rollo

(Hrolf) was made the first Duke of Normandy by the Carolingian king Charles the Simple in exchange for his allegiance and his help in expelling other Vikings. This was the beginning of the amazing ascent and worldwide expansion of the Normans.

21

The people called Rus in early Russian chronicles were possibly of mixed origin, but certainly included Swedish Viking traders. The city of Novgorod, shown here, was traditionally founded in about 860 by the Rus chieftain Rurick, supposedly also the ancestor of the great dynasty that came to

22

rule farther south in Kiev. In 839 the Rus sent ambassadors to the court of the Byzantine emperor; by the 860s they had begun attacking his capital, Constantinople. Viking trade in eastern Europe was extensive; Islamic goods and coins flowed into Scandinavia from southwestern and central Asia.

23

About 985, Eric (Eirik) the Red, who had been outlawed from both Norway and Iceland, discovered Greenland and founded a colony on the south coast. About fifteen years later, his son Leif followed up a chance sighting of new lands to the southwest with a planned exploration; settlement followed later. Controversy rages over exactly which areas of North America the Vikings knew as Vinland (almost

surely meaning "grape country"), Markland ("forest country") and other names. Certainly L'Anse aux Meadows on Newfoundland is a true Viking site. This drawing is based on an 1893 painting by the Norwegian artist Christian Krohg depicting the Viking discovery of America.

The Vikings' first encounters with the native people of North America, whom they called Skraelings, were friendly. The Norsemen traded woven cloth and other goods for furs. Conflict developed, however, and after a few years the Greenlanders were forced to abandon their settlements.

26

Another term for Norsemen in eastern Europe was Varangians. After the Viking presence in Russia diminished, some Norsemen were employed by Byzantine emperors, from about the year 1000 on, as elite bodyguards—the famous Varangian Guard, of which Harold Hardraade (later king of Norway and invader of England) was a member. The Vikings reached Athens, too: a large marble lion, found in the harbor of Piraeus and now at the entrance to the Arsenal in Venice, bears a carved runic graffito on its shoulder.

During the Viking period, Denmark, Norway and Sweden were steadily becoming unified nations under powerful monarchs—not without frequent conflicts, both internal and external. In or about the year 1000 the Norwegian king Olaf Tryggvason was defeated and killed in the sea battle of Svolder (Swold) in the Baltic by a coalition of Swedes under their king Olaf Skötkonung and the Danes under the forceful Svein (Sweyn) Forkbeard. During sea fighting, masts were taken down and ships were often lashed together like floating fortresses.

Svein Forkbeard, the Danish king, was also successful in England. The successors of Alfred the Great were not always as resolute as Alfred had been. Anglo-Saxon kings paid the Norsemen huge sums of money and goods in tribute (known as Danegeld), but invasions still continued. Finally in 1013 Svein conquered the south of England. The drawing shows a Viking attack on a fortified Anglo-Saxon *tun* (town). Denmark and England were then joined in one kingdom until 1042, the most famous ruler in this period being Svein's son Canute (Knut).

29

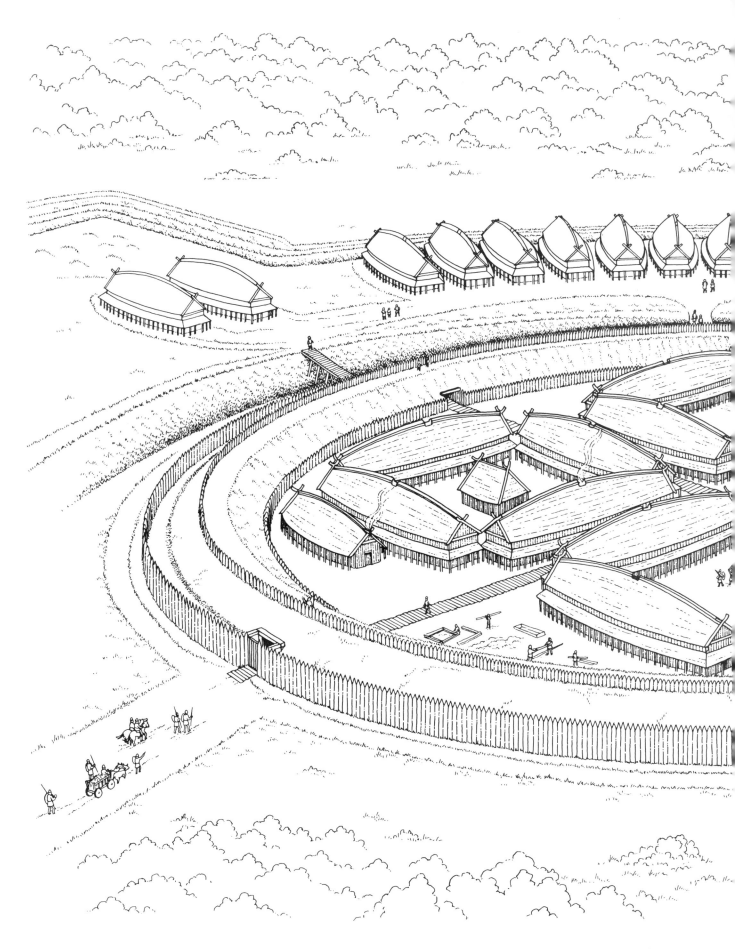

In order to maintain control in Denmark while they pursued their adventures abroad, Svein and Canute (and even earlier Danish kings) established an elaborate system of fortified camps holding garrisons of up to 1,200 men each. These regional strongholds had earthen walls strengthened by

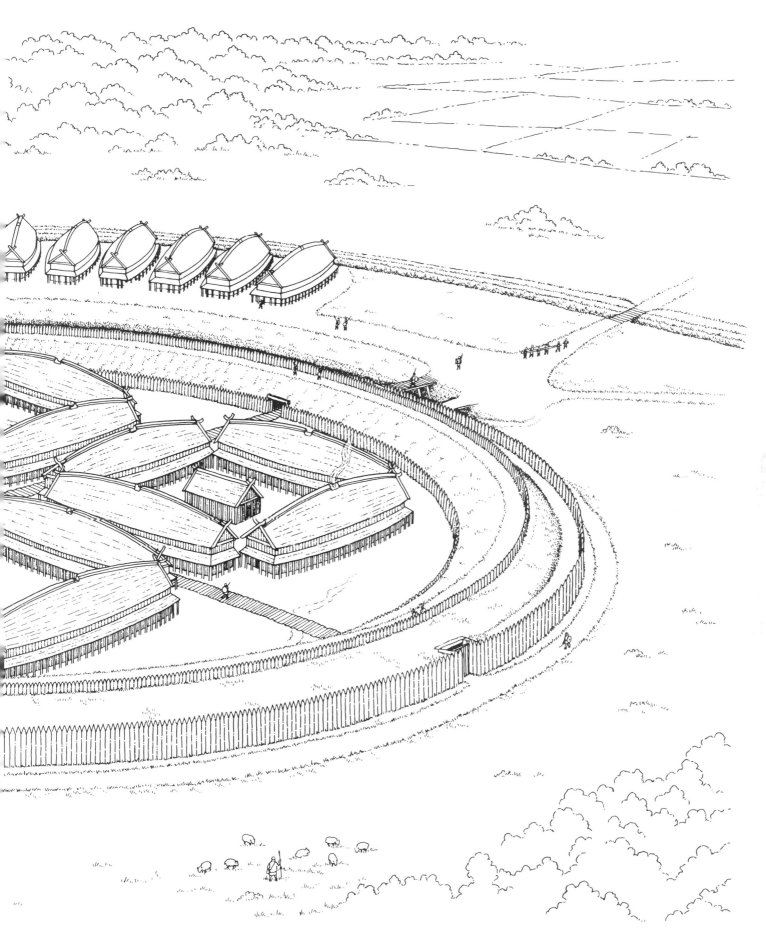

timber palisades. Illustrated is the camp at Trelleborg. The boat-shaped buildings in the background are barracks.

The last major Viking adventure in England—seen by some historians as the effective end of the Viking Age—was the Norwegian king Harald Hardraade's invasion in 1066 as a claimant to the throne on the death of Edward the Confessor. The new Anglo-Saxon king Harold Godwinsson defeated Harald at Stamford Bridge in Yorkshire on September 25 (see illustration), only to succumb to the Normans, led by William the Conqueror, at Hastings on the south coast nineteen days later.

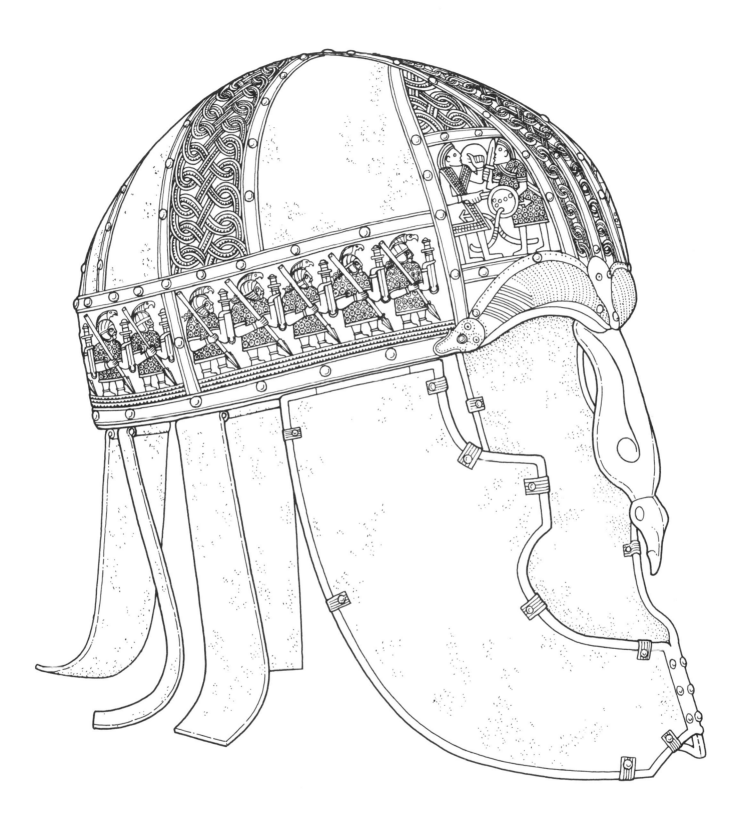

The arts, crafts and daily life of the Vikings had developed gradually over several centuries, from at least late Roman times onward. One of the finest objects preserved from immediately pre-Viking times is this magnificent bronze-ornamented iron helmet from the Vendel culture in the Uppland region of Sweden. The life and civilization of the pre-Viking era in Sweden are clearly reflected in the Old English epic poem *Beowulf*, composed in the eighth century.

Viking home life centered around the hearth in a long hall. Benches along the sides served as beds for most of the household. Smoke escaped through a small vent in the roof. Storytelling (seen here) was a favorite entertainment. In royal and noble homes, feasting was often spectacular.

Woolen cloth was the most important textile manufactured by the Vikings. It was woven on standing looms, the warp threads being kept straight by stone or clay weights. The woman in this picture is beating the thread into place with a wooden "weaving sword." Viking women not only directed household affairs; they had much more independence as property owners and greater power in divorce procedures than their European sisters of the time.

The armorer, or weaponsmith, forged swords, battleaxes and spears. He also made helmets, chain
mail and shields for defense.

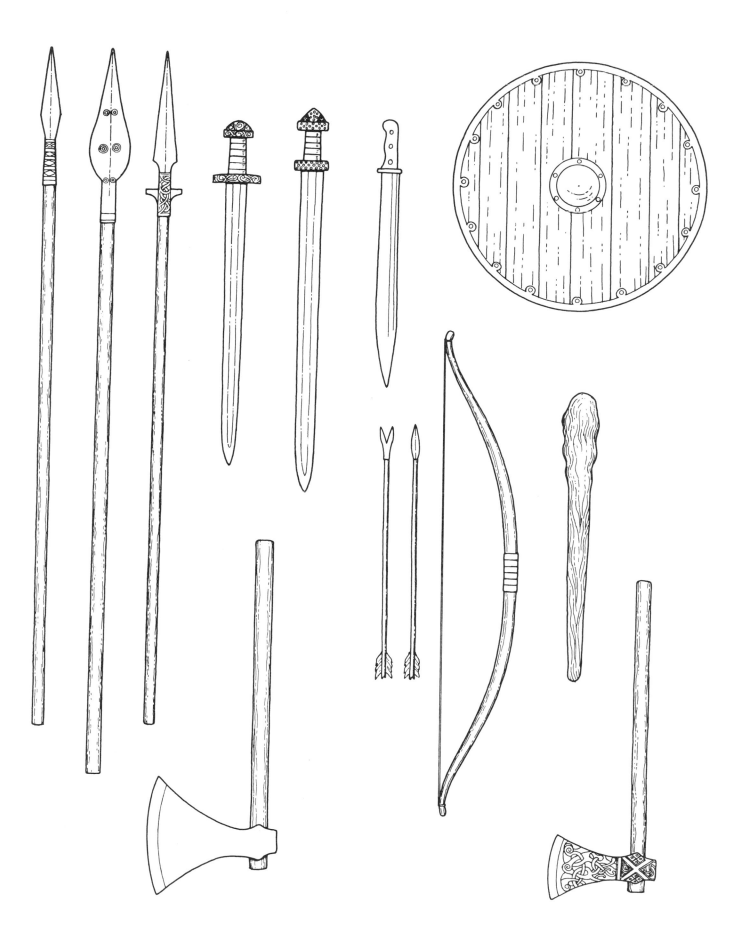

Viking weapons were often decorated with inlays of silver wire and niello (a black alloy). The shields were brightly painted.

The Vikings were excellent horsemen, and a warrior's horse was sometimes buried with him. Only a wealthy chieftain like the one pictured could afford a shirt of chain mail. Stirrups, invented in the Far East about 200 B.C., reached Europe in the eighth century A.D. and were known in Viking Scandinavia. The Normans, of Viking origin, made decisive use of their heavy cavalry in their conquest of England in 1066.

Personal disputes between Norsemen were often settled by combat, sometimes taking the form of an isolated duel on a small offshore island. This duel was called a *holmganga* ("island-going"). Killings and revenges often escalated into long-running feuds between families, although a system was devised by which survivors could be compensated financially for the loss of kinsmen.

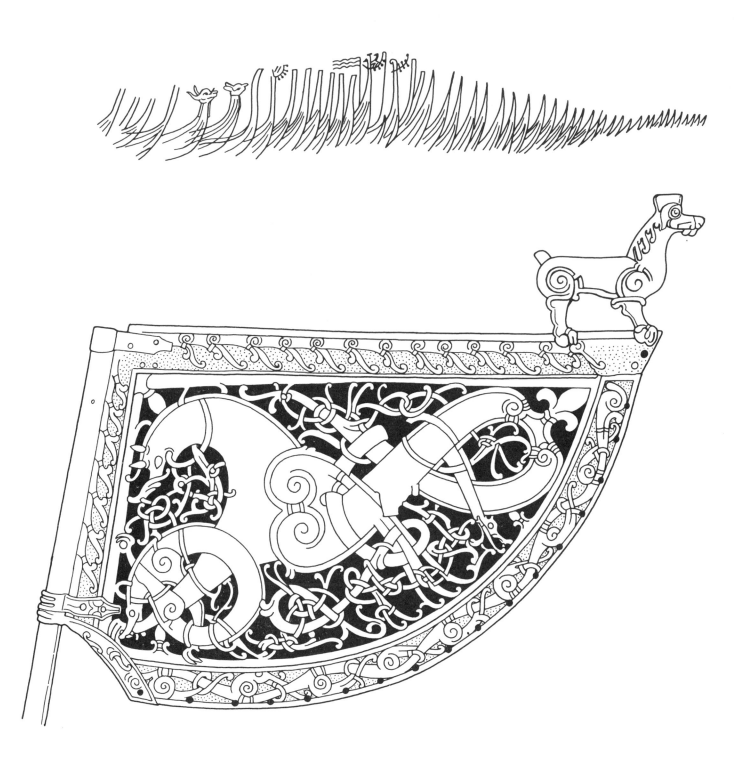

The ship—most prized possession of the Viking and often colorfully named (*Long Dragon, Crane, Long Serpent*)—was sometimes lavishly decorated. The upper drawing, depicting a Viking fleet with ornamented prows, is based on a wood carving excavated at Bergen, Norway. Below that is a gilt-bronze weather vane that ornamented either the masthead or the prow of a longship; it represents a "great beast" and probably dates from the eleventh century.

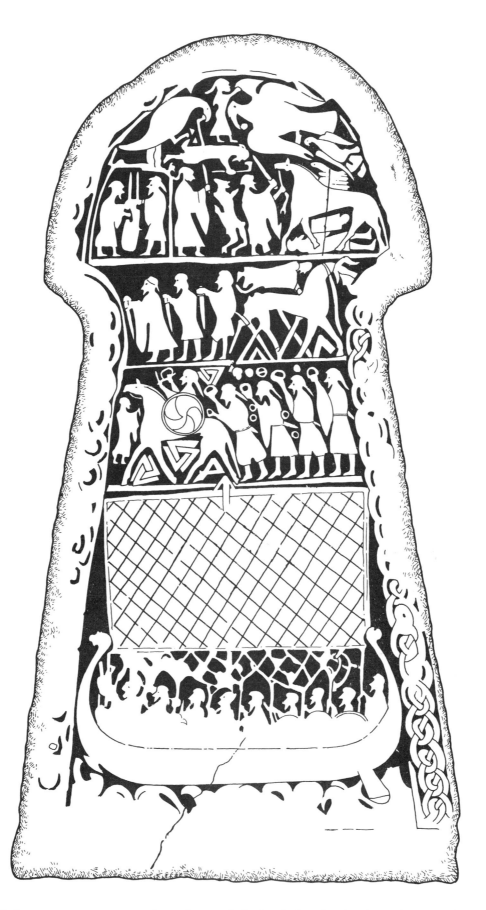

An eighth-century picture stone from the Swedish island of Gotland in the Baltic Sea. This limestone shaft was originally about eleven feet high, but some two feet of it are now missing. The top level depicts a battle; the next level, probably a burial; the scene below that probably represents fallen Vikings entering Valhalla, the special afterlife abode of heroes; at the bottom is a warship. Such stones were often erected as memorials of people or events.

The Norse religion had many gods and goddesses, each with special powers for specific occasions and needs. UPPER LEFT: Odin (god of creation, war and poetry) on his eight-legged horse Sleipnir. UPPER RIGHT: Thor (god of thunder) with his magic hammer, or Frey (god of fertility); a three-inch-high bronze statuette. LOWER LEFT: Bronze statuette of Frey from Rällinge, Sweden. LOWER RIGHT: Pendant depicting a woman with a drinking horn, possibly a Valkyrie (celestial warrior maiden) welcoming a fallen hero to Valhalla.

f u th o r k h n i a s t b m l R

A granite block with runic inscriptions from the Södermanland province of Sweden. The stone is five feet, three inches high. Runes were letter forms used at the time in many areas of Europe for writing the local language (Norse, Old English, etc.). Their angular form was suited to their original use: against-the-grain incisions on wood. The sixteen-sign alphabet shown is the simplified but imperfect one used in Denmark in the Viking age. The equivalent in our alphabet appears below each sign ("th" pronounced as in "thin," "R" standing for a special r-sound).

Aside from court poetry, composed in many Viking lands, the chief form of literature was the prose sagas—mostly royal, local or family histories—which were written mainly in Iceland from the eleventh through the fourteenth centuries. In the foreground above is Snorri Sturluson (1179–1241), probably the greatest saga writer. In the background is the climactic scene—the burning of Njal's home, with the family inside—from *Njal's Saga* (anonymous, ca. 1280; about a widespread family feud), often considered the finest single saga.

Another excellent saga, and one that may have been written by Snorri, is *Egil's Saga* (ca. 1230). Its hero, Egil Skallagrimsson, was a major poet as well as a ruthless fighting man; he lived from about 910 to 990. The illustration shows the scene from the saga in which Egil carries the body of his drowned son Bodvar to the family burial mound. Subsequently Egil composed his finest poem, "Lament for My Sons," which is included in the saga.

The Scandinavian countries were progressively Christianized during the tenth and eleventh centuries. The twelfth and thirteenth centuries in Norway saw the construction of numerous stave churches, outstanding timber buildings (with walls of upright planks) much more elaborate than most Viking architecture had been. Illustrated is the church at Borgund (ca. 1200), in which the dragon heads on the gables hark back to pagan days.

The doorway of another Norwegian stave church is richly carved with interlacing animal and floral ornament. Birds, snakes and dragons intertwine their necks, bodies and legs in fantastic patterns inspired by earlier Viking art.

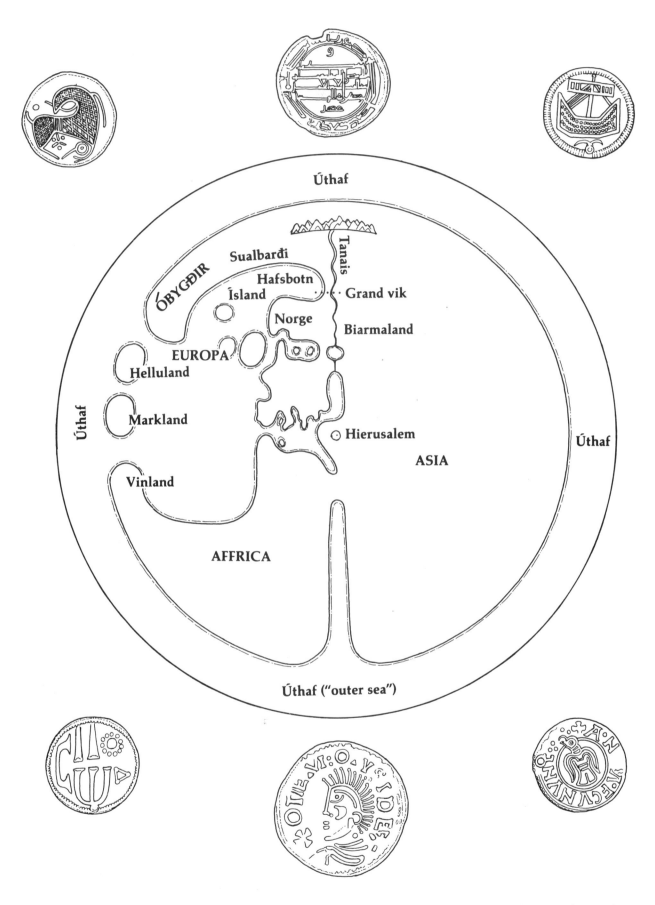

Úthaf

Úthaf

Úthaf

Úthaf ("outer sea")

ÓBYGÐIR Sualbarði

Hafsbotn

Ísland

Norge

EUROPA

Helluland

Markland

Vinland

AFFRICA

Tanais

Grand vik

Biarmaland

Hierusalem

ASIA

As the map in the center shows, the Vikings conceived of the world as one large landmass and several islands in a great endless sea. Also illustrated are a few of the types of coins found in Viking graves. At the top left is an early coin minted at Hedeby, Denmark, ca. 800–825. Next to it is an Islamic coin acquired through commerce. At the bottom right is a silver penny (showing a raven) from the Viking kingdom of York, England, ca. 940.